Equal Shmequal

by Virginia Kroll • illustrated by Philomena O'Neill

Charlesbridge

For my half dozen, who are divided equally: Sara, Hannah,
and Katya, the girls; and Seth, Joshua, and Noah, the boys — V.K.

For Maura and Bill — P.O.

Text copyright ©2005 by Virginia Kroll
Illustrations copyright ©2005 by Philomena O'Neill
All rights reserved, including the right of reproduction in whole or in part in any form.
Charlesbridge and colophon are registered trademarks of Charlesbridge Publishing, Inc.
Published by Charlesbridge, 85 Main Street, Watertown, MA 02472
(617) 926-0329 • www.charlesbridge.com

Library of Congress Cataloging-in-Publication Data
Kroll, Virginia L.
  Equal shmequal / by Virginia Kroll ; illustrated by Philomena O'Neill.
    p. cm.
Summary: In order to have fun at a game of tug-of-war, forest animals
balance the teams by using a see-saw. Includes nonfiction math notes for
meanings of equal.
  ISBN 1-57091-891-0 (reinforced for library use) -- ISBN 1-57091-892-9 (softcover)
  [1. Forest animals--Fiction. 2. Equations--Fiction. 3. Mathematics--Fiction.] I. O'Neill, Philomena, ill. II. Title.
PZ7.K9227Eq 2005
[E]--dc22
                                    2004023051

Printed in Korea
(hc) 10 9 8 7 6 5 4 3 2 1   (sc) 10 9 8 7 6 5 4 3 2 1

A little brown mouse sat under a leaf watching a school picnic. The children finished eating and began to play. Some played tag. Some chose teams for a game.

"The two sides have to be equal!" one of them shouted.

The children pulled on the ends of a rope.
One team was pulled over a line. The other
team cheered, "Hooray! We won, we won!"

Then one of the teachers called to the
children. They all got into a big yellow
bus that drove off down the road.

All was quiet.

"Hmm. That looked like fun. Hey, Bear!" called Mouse. "Come out and play!"

Bear walked out from the trees. "What do you want to play?"

"It's a game," squeaked Mouse. "You take one end of the rope and I take the other. We both pull to see who wins!"

5

Bear gave the rope a mighty yank. Mouse flew across the field. She landed on the ground with a thump.

"Hey," said Bear. "Where did you go?"

"No fair!" squealed Mouse. She picked herself up.
"I forgot that teams have to be *equal*."

"Equal shmequal!" said Bear.

Suddenly, sharp claws grabbed Mouse. It was Bobcat.
"Gotcha!" he snarled.

"Help!" squealed Mouse.

Bear stood up on his hind legs and growled,
"Let Mouse go right now!"

Bobcat whimpered. "I just want to join the game. See, Wolf's right here! He wants to play too."

Wolf stepped out into the open.

Mouse brushed off her fur. She said in her bravest voice, "Of course you guys can play. Everyone can play as long as the teams are equal."

"Equal shmequal," said Bear.
He reached into one of the trash cans
and pulled out a half-eaten sandwich.

Rabbit hopped into the field. "Can we play too?" Rabbit asked.

Box Turtle plodded close behind.
"What does equal mean, anyway?"
he asked.

"'Equal' means 'fair,'" explained Mouse.
"We should divide into two equal teams somehow."

"Equal shmequal," Bear mumbled
with a mouthful of chocolate cake.

"Let's try meat-eaters against
plant-eaters," said Rabbit.
"That would be fair."

"What about Turtle and me?"
asked Mouse. "We eat anything
small enough."

"Well," said Rabbit, "what are your favorite foods?"

Mouse replied, "I like blackberries best!"

"I eat mostly bugs," said Turtle, "but my favorite food is dandelions."

"If you like plants best, you belong on my team," said Rabbit.

"So it's animals that eat only meat against the rest of us."

Bobcat laughed. "You think this is equal? Ha!"

With just one hard pull, he and Wolf yanked Mouse, Rabbit, and Turtle across the line. They landed in a heap.

"That wasn't equal," Turtle complained, peeking from his shell.

Bobcat said, "Everyone with fur, go to one side.
Everyone without fur, go to the other." But that
left only Turtle on a team. That couldn't be equal!

"Does anyone know what halves are?" Rabbit asked.
"I've heard the farmer talking about halves."

"Halves are what you get when you make two
groups with the same number," Mouse said.
"We can't make halves because there are five of us."

Just then Mouse saw hooves behind a bush.
"Hey," she said. "Maybe Deer will want to play.
Then we can make halves."

Deer slowly stepped out of the woods. "It looks like fun," she said, "but I want to keep an eye on Wolf and Bobcat. I'll pull from behind them."

The animals lined up, three on one side and three on the other. They pulled, but once again, Mouse, Rabbit, and Turtle were easily dragged over the line.

"No fair!" complained Rabbit. "They're all big, and we're all small, so it isn't equal at all."

"You're right," said Mouse. "The numbers are equal, but that doesn't make the teams equal."

"Equal shmequal!" Bear exclaimed, finishing off a piece of pizza.

The animals scowled at each other.
Everyone began talking at the same time.

"It's no fair, you're so much bigger…"

"You're just mad because you lost…"

"You don't care if the teams are
equal as long as you win…"

Mouse sat by herself and tried to think of a new idea.
She tapped a tiny foot and twirled a wiry whisker.

"Listen," said Mouse. "Listen up!" she said louder.
"I have an idea!"

The animals stopped fighting. "Well?" asked Bobcat.
"What's your great idea?"

"I thought that instead of equal *numbers*," she explained,
"our teams could have equal weights. We could use the
seesaw to figure it out."

"Look," said Mouse. "When what's on one side of the seesaw is equal to what's on the other side, the seesaw balances. You can tell because it's straight across."

"Okay," said Turtle. "Let me get on first, since I can't jump."

He walked onto the end of the seesaw touching the ground.

"I'll get on the other side," Wolf said.

Wolf jumped onto the center of the seesaw and made
his way to the end.

Turtle was lifted high into the air.
He looked down the long way to the ground
and tried not to be scared.

Deer got up on Turtle's side.
Their side sank down, and Wolf rose up into the air.

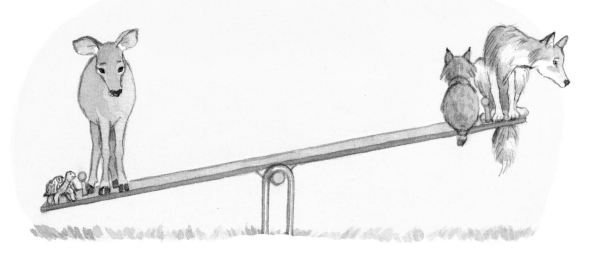

"I'm next!" shouted Bobcat. He got onto Wolf's side,
but Wolf and Bobcat together were still up in the air.

With a mighty hop, Rabbit landed in front of Bobcat.
Now the seesaw was almost balanced.

"Come on!" shouted Rabbit. "You're the last one, Mouse!"

Mouse scampered up next to Deer. The seesaw teetered
back and forth before resting perfectly straight across.
The teams were balanced.

"We did it! We're equal!" Mouse squeaked.

Then Bear looked up from his crumbs
and ran over roaring, "Wait for *me*!"

He jumped on and down went his side
of the seesaw with a bump.

Deer, Mouse, and Turtle went flying into the air.

"Oops," said Bear. "I guess it's not equal anymore."

23

"We can get this right," Mouse said cheerfully. "Let's try again. Bear, get on first."

Bear sat on one end with the other end high in the air.

Bobcat offered to get on the high side first. "If I fall, I'll land on my feet. Cats always do!"

The rest of the animals got on. Each one made Bear's side lift a little.

Finally, all the animals
were on except Mouse. "Come on!"
shouted Rabbit. "We're almost equal!"

Mouse jumped onto the middle of the seesaw.
Bear's side was higher,
so she walked
toward him.

The seesaw was
perfectly balanced.

They jumped off one by one and picked up the rope.
Bear and Mouse were on one side of the line and all
the other animals were on the other.

"Okay," said Mouse. "Now the teams have equal weight.
Whichever team pulls the other across this line wins!"

26

Bear and Mouse pulled. Turtle, Rabbit, Bobcat, Wolf, and Deer pulled back. "I'm bigger than all of you," said Bear. "I'll win!"

"Come on," said Rabbit to her teammates. "There are more of us. Pull harder!"

They pulled and tugged, but neither team moved an inch.

"What if no one can win?" asked Rabbit.

Suddenly, they heard a loud buzzing overhead. "Bees!" shouted Bear. "There must be honey nearby!" He took one paw off the rope to point at the swarm of bees.

Just then, the other team gave a mighty pull and Bear stepped over the line.

"Hooray!" said Rabbit. "We won! We won!"

"But the teams were equal," said Deer. "How did we win?"

"What really matters is equal *effort*," said Mouse.

"When we all pulled our hardest, the effort was equal.
That's why no one could win. But when Bear saw the bees,
he forgot to pull. The effort wasn't equal anymore."

"Equal shmequal," said Bear. "I want some honey."

Mouse laughed. "Time for a honey break!" she said.

The animals followed the bees to their hive in a tree.
There was more than enough honey for everyone,
and they shared it equally.

What It Means to Be Equal

In math, to be equal means to have parts that are the same in weight, size, quantity, or other measure.

In art, equal can mean symmetrical, which means you can draw a line through the middle of a picture and one half will look just like the other half.

In law, equal means having the same opportunities, rights, and privileges.

In team sports, the teams have equal numbers. All the players must give their best effort in order to have the best chance of winning.